# SCIENCE AND TECHNOLOGY

Ian Graham

QEB Publishing

Copyright © QEB Publishing, Inc. 2008

Published in the United States by
QEB Publishing, Inc.
23062 La Cadena Drive
Laguna Hills, CA 92653

www.qeb-publishing.com

Library of Congress Control Number: 2008012582

ISBN 978 1 59566 601 7

Printed and bound in the United States


**Author** Ian Graham
**Consultant** Sue Becklake
**Editor** Amanda Askew
**Designer** Gaspard de Beauvais
**Picture Researcher** Maria Joannou
**Illustrator** Richard Burgess


**Publisher** Steve Evans
**Creative Director** Zeta Davies


**Picture credits** (t=top, b=bottom, l=left, r=right)
**Corbis** Bettmann 10t, Remi Benali 25, Roger Ressmeyer 8–9
**Getty Images** China Photos13, Li Shaowen/ChinaFotoPress 22b,
Luis Gene/AFP Photo 23, Spencer Platt 4b, Terry Smith//Time Life
Pictures 26b
**iRobot** 28r
**Istockphoto** 10–11, 10b
**Livermore National Laboratory** 14b
**NASA** 5, 11, 14t, 16l, 17r, 18–19, 18b, 19t, ESA/JPL/Arizona State
University 8l, JPL/Cornell University 16–17
**Photolibrary Philippe Pons/Photononstop** 22t
**Rex Features** 4t, 20–21, 29, Sipa Press 21b
**Science Photo Library** Andrew Lambert Photography 12–13,
Colin Cuthbert 26t, Dale Boyer/NASA 14–15, David Parker 9r,
Fermi National Accelerator Laboratory 21t, Jim Varney 27,
Mauro Fermariello 7b, Pascal Goetgheluck 24, Roger Harris 28l,
Volker Steger/Peter Arnold Inc 6b
**Shutterstock** 6–7, 7t, 24–25

Words in **bold** can be found in
the glossary on page 30.

# Contents

# EXPLORING SCIENCE

**People have tried to understand the Earth and the Universe around them for thousands of years. During that time, they have invented many instruments to collect more and more information about how nature works.**

## Technology

Science is the study of the natural world. Technology is the use of science to make things and solve problems. A new piece of technology is an invention. All sorts of inventions, from televisions and computers to cars and planes, are based on scientific discoveries.

This soccer ball was invented with technology inside to tell the referee if it crosses the goal line.

Ordinary people may be able to take short trips into space by 2010 with Virgin Galactic.

## Space exploration

People have been traveling into space since 1961. Most of them were professional **astronauts**. Now, several companies are developing **spacecraft** to carry tourists into space. A typical flight would last two to three hours and the passengers would be weightless for a few minutes.

# SCIENCE AND TECHNOLOGY INVENTIONS

*c.*1600 **Microscope**
*c.*1608 **Telescope**
1668 **Reflecting telescope**
1928 **Particle accelerator**
1931 **Electron microscope**
1937 **Radio telescope**
1942 **Nuclear reactor**
1945 **Electronic computer**
1959 **Industrial robot**
1959 **Space probe**
1960 **Laser**
1971 **Space station**
1984 **Genetic fingerprinting**
1990 **Hubble Space Telescope**

## Smart machines

Most machines do only the simple things that they were designed to do. Now there are machines that can make decisions, see, speak, or understand what is said to them.

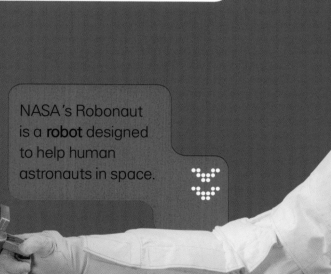

NASA's Robonaut is a **robot** designed to help human astronauts in space.

# INVISIBLE WORLD

When the microscope was invented in about 1600, it revealed a new world of tiny creatures that had never been seen before. It showed the bugs that make people sick. It also showed the cells that living things are made of.

## Bending rays

Microscopes use specially shaped blocks of glass called **lenses** to bend light rays so that small things look bigger. The first lenses were probably made in Arabia about 1,000 years ago. When one lens on its own is used to make small things look bigger, it is called a simple microscope. When two or more lenses are used, they form a compound microscope.

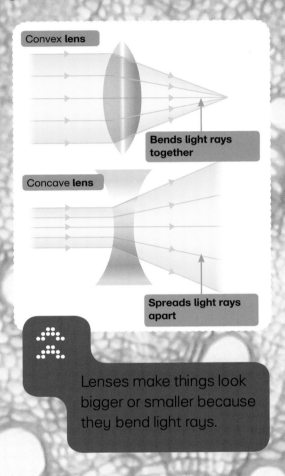

Convex **lens**

Bends light rays together

Concave **lens**

Spreads light rays apart

The microscopes made by Antonie van Leeuwenhoek had a lens the size of a water droplet. It was held between two metal plates.

Lenses make things look bigger or smaller because they bend light rays.

## Simple and better

In the 1670s, Dutch draper Antonie van Leeuwenhoek made simple microscopes from one high-power lens that could **magnify** something more than 250 times. Later, higher-quality lenses enabled scientists to make more powerful compound microscopes.

Different lenses can be used in a modern microscope to make things look bigger and bigger.

## More power

The compound microscope was invented by Dutch spectacle maker Zacharias Janssen in the late 1590s when he put two lenses together in a tube. Today, scientists use more powerful compound microscopes to magnify things up to about 2,000 times.

Some electron microscopes are so powerful that they can see atoms, the particles of matter that everything is made of.

## DID YOU KNOW?

**Robert Hooke was the first important scientist to write a book about the amazing things he saw through a microscope. His book was called *Micrographia*. When people saw it in 1665, they were amazed by drawings of the strange things he had seen.**

## *Electron microscopes*

The microscopes used by most scientists today magnify things a few hundred times. The most powerful microscopes can magnify something up to two million times. Instead of light, they use a beam of **electrons**. The **electron microscope** was invented by German engineers Ernst Ruska and Max Knoll in 1931.

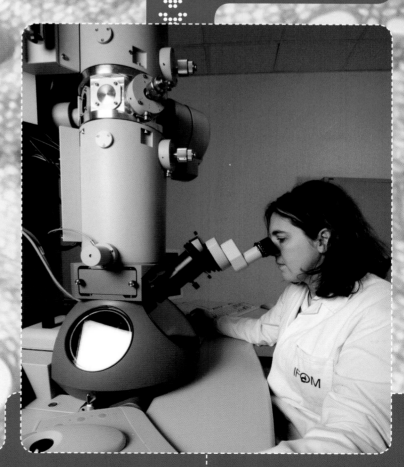

# SEEING FURTHER

Telescopes make faraway objects look closer and bigger. Astronomers have used them for the past 400 years to look into space and learn more about the Universe.

## Telescopes

The first telescope was probably made by Dutch spectacle maker Hans Lippershey in *c.*1608. The famous Italian scientist Galileo Galilei heard about Lippershey's invention and then made his own telescopes. Using them, he discovered four moons going round the planet Jupiter. They are known as the Galilean moons.

## Newton's mirrors

To build more powerful telescopes, bigger lenses were needed. Big lenses were difficult to make in the 1600s. In 1668, English scientist Sir Isaac Newton invented a new type of telescope that did not need a big lens. Instead, it had a curved mirror. Mirrors were easier to make.

Extremely clear pictures are taken by the Hubble Space Telescope. It orbits the Earth about 375 miles above the ground.

Modern telescopes have a big curved mirror to collect lots of light and focus it to make a sharp picture. A dome protects the telescope from the weather.

## Radio pictures

In 1931, U.S. physicist Karl Jansky discovered that some of the crackles and hisses people heard on their radio sets were caused by radio waves from space. Another U.S. scientist Grote Reber read about Jansky's work. In 1937, Reber built the first radio telescope to study these space waves. It had a metal dish 31.4 feet across. The biggest radio telescope dish today is 1,000 feet across!

This radio telescope is built in a natural bowl-shaped hollow in the ground near Arecibo on the Caribbean island of Puerto Rico.

## DID YOU KNOW?

Soon after the Hubble Space Telescope was launched in 1990, scientists discovered that its big mirror had been made the wrong shape and its pictures were blurred! In 1993, astronauts visited the telescope and fitted extra mirrors to fix the problem.

# GOING NUCLEAR

Atoms, **the particles of** matter **everything is made of, contain a lot of** energy. **Nuclear power stations use this energy to make electricity. About one-fifth of all the world's electricity is made in this way.**

## The first pile

Atoms are made to give up their energy inside a **nuclear reactor**. The first successful nuclear reactor was built by Italian scientist Enrico Fermi. He built it on a squash court at the University of Chicago in 1942. It was called an atomic pile because of the way it was built.

This scale model shows the first atomic pile built by Enrico Fermi and his team.

Atomic pile

## First nuclear power station

The first large commercial nuclear power station in the world was Calder Hall in Cumbria, England. On October 17, 1956, Queen Elizabeth II pressed the switch to start the flow of electricity from Calder Hall to people's homes.

The dome of a nuclear power station contains the nuclear reactor where the nuclear fuel is kept. It stops dangerous radiation from getting out should there be an accident.

probe is on its way to a small faraway world called Pluto. *New Horizon's* instruments are powered by electricity from a nuclear electricity generator.

## *Nuclear power in space*

Most space probes make the electricity they need from sunlight. Space probes that go far from the Sun cannot do this because there is not enough sunlight. NASA invented a nuclear-powered electricity **generator** for space probes. It is called a radio-isotope thermoelectric generator, or RTG. It was tested in space for the first time on a satellite called Transit 4A in 1961.

# LASERS

**A laser is a device that produces an intense beam of pure light. Lasers are used in scientific research, industry, DVD players, communications, and medicine.**

## Laser light

Light is made of tiny waves of energy. The color of light depends on the length of the waves. Red light is made of the longest waves. Blue light has the shortest waves. Sunlight contains all the colors of the rainbow and the waves are jumbled up together. The light in a laser is made of waves that are all the same length and traveling in the same direction in step with each other.

A ruby laser uses a bright flash of light to make a powerful beam.

Flash tube

Partly silvered mirror

Ruby rod

Mirror

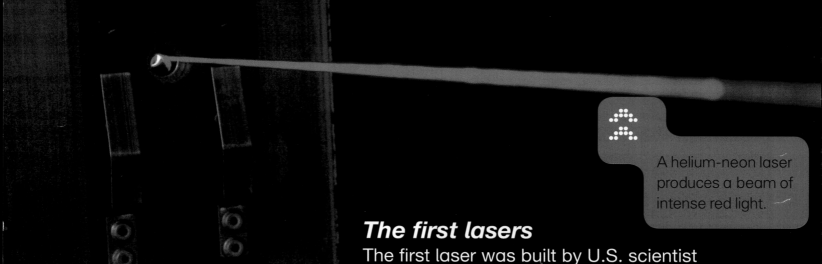

A helium-neon laser produces a beam of intense red light.

## The first lasers

The first laser was built by U.S. scientist Theodore Maiman in 1960. It produced flashes of laser light. Later that year, Iranian scientist Ali Javan and U.S. scientists William Bennett and Donald Herriott built the first helium-neon gas laser. It produced a steady beam of red light instead of flashes.

## *Medical lasers*

In medicine, lasers are used to cut like a knife and to destroy harmful **cells**. They work by heating cells until they burn away. A different type of laser is used for operations on the front of the eye. Heating cannot be used here because it would make the clear part of the eye cloudy and destroy the eyesight. Instead, an excimer laser is used. It uses just enough energy to break cells apart without heating them. American eye specialist Steven Trokel carried out this type of laser eye surgery for the first time in 1987.

As well as operating on the front of the eye, lasers are also used to repair leaky blood vessels and other damage at the back of the eye.

Cornea

Pupil

Laser beam

Lens

This laser is changing the shape of the front of an eye to cure short-sightedness.

## DID YOU KNOW?

When astronauts landed on the Moon, they placed a special reflector on its dusty surface. A laser fired from the Earth hit the reflector and bounced back to Earth. The time the light took to go to the Moon and back allowed scientists to work out the distance between the Earth and Moon very accurately.

# SUPERCOMPUTERS

**Supercomputers are the fastest and most powerful computers in the world. They are put to work on the most difficult problems in science and engineering.**

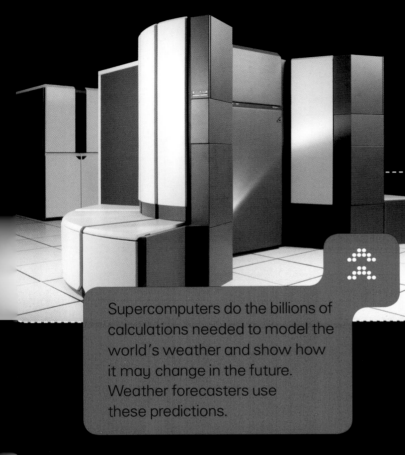

### The first supercomputer

The supercomputer was invented in the 1960s. The first one was Control Data Corporation's CDC 6600. It could work out about three million sums in one second—three times more calculations than the next fastest computer at that time.

Supercomputers do the billions of calculations needed to model the world's weather and show how it may change in the future. Weather forecasters use these predictions.

### Super power

At the end of 2007, the fastest supercomputer in the world was the IBM Blue Gene/L. In November 2007, it reached a new top speed of 478 trillion calculations a second. A trillion is a thousand billion. A new Blue Gene supercomputer, the Blue Gene/P, is being built to work out more than 1,000 trillion calculations a second.

Most computers have one main processing chip that runs the computer. Supercomputers have lots of processors. Blue Gene/L has about 131,000 processors.

## *Using supercomputers*

Blue Gene/L and other supercomputers today work by splitting up a large, complicated problem into lots of small problems. Then different parts of the computer work on all the small problems at the same time. This is called parallel processing. The parallel computer was invented in the 1960s. The first one was called Iliac-IV. NASA started using it in 1972.

This picture was drawn by a supercomputer to show how air flows around a jet plane. Aircraft designers need to know about this to make a plane the best possible shape.

## DID YOU KNOW?

If you could do one sum every five seconds on your pocket calculator and keep going for eight hours a day, how long do you think it would take you to do as many calculations as the fastest supercomputer can do in one second? A year? Ten years? No, you would need 227 million years!

# SPACE PROBES

A space probe is an unmanned spacecraft sent away from Earth to collect information for scientists. A space probe may fly past a planet or Moon, go into orbit around it, or land on it.

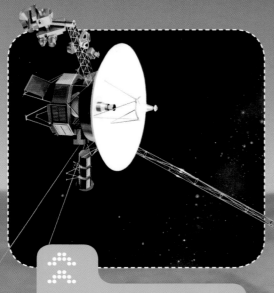

### *First flybys*

The first space probe, *Luna 1*, was launched in 1959 by the Soviet Union. It was the first spacecraft to escape from the Earth's pull of **gravity** and fly away past the Moon. In 1977, NASA sent two Voyager space probes to visit the most distant planets in the Solar System. *Voyager 1* flew past Jupiter and Saturn. *Voyager 2* visited these planets plus Uranus and Neptune. The Voyagers sent back the first close-up photographs of these planets.

The *Voyager 2* space probe flew past all four of the outer planets in the 1970s and 1980s.

## DID YOU KNOW?

The *Voyager 1* space probe is now the furthest manmade object from Earth. It is 9.7 billion miles away. Its mission was supposed to last five years, but it is still working after 30 years! It should keep going until it runs out of electrical power in about 2020.

## Galileo *space probe*

A space probe has more time to study a planet if it goes into orbit around the planet instead of flying past it. In 1995, after a six-year flight from Earth, the *Galileo* space probe went into orbit around the giant planet Jupiter. It spent eight years circling Jupiter.

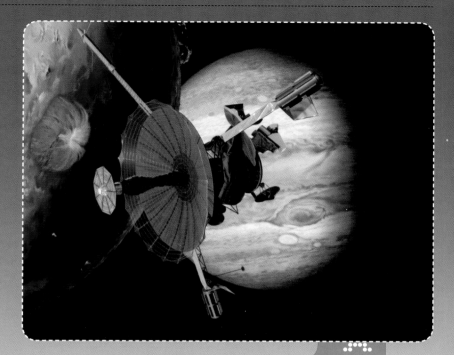

The *Galileo* space probe went around Jupiter 35 times and sent 14,000 photographs back to Earth. During its 14-year mission, it traveled a total of 2.8 billion miles.

## *Lander*

Space probes that land on another planet are called landers. They usually stay in one spot, but some landers carry small electric vehicles called rovers. A rover moves around studying rocks and soil in different places. In 2004, two rovers called *Spirit* and *Opportunity* landed on the red planet, Mars.

The Mars rovers are powered by electricity from solar panels, which are made from solar cells that were invented in the 1940s by U.S. inventor Russell Ohl.

# SPACE STATIONS

**Manned spacecraft usually go into space for a few days or weeks and then come back to Earth.** Space stations are different. They are manned spacecraft that stay in space all the time. Astronauts visit a space station and live there until the next crew arrives to take over.

People live and work in the tube-shaped parts of the International Space Station. These parts are called modules.

## The first space stations

People have written stories about space stations since the 1860s. The name "space station" was invented by Romanian-born scientist Herman Oberth in 1923. The Soviet Union built the first space station, Salyut 1, and launched it into space in 1971. It was the first of seven Salyut space stations. The first U.S. space station, Skylab, was launched in 1973.

The U.S. Skylab space station was built from an old Apollo Moon-rocket. It was as big inside as a small house.

Destiny laboratory

Robot arm

## Building site in space

In 1986, the Soviet Union launched a new type of space station called Mir. It was the first space station that was launched in pieces and put together in space. The U.S. space shuttle was able to dock with Mir, so U.S. astronauts could visit it.

Some astronauts spent a year or more living in the Mir space station.

**Solar panel**

**Zvezda Service Module**

## DID YOU KNOW?

In 1997, an unmanned spacecraft went out of control as it headed toward Mir space station and crashed into it. It punched a hole in Mir and air started leaking out. The astronauts sealed off that part to stop the space station from losing all of its air.

**Soyuz spacecraft**

## Space giant

The biggest structure ever built in space is being put together now by 16 countries including the United States, Russia, Canada, and Japan. It's the International Space Station. The first part was launched in 1998. About 40 spaceflights and 160 spacewalks will be needed to launch all the other parts and finish building the station by about 2010. Astronauts have lived on board the International Space Station since 2000.

# ATOM SMASHERS

**Particles are small pieces of matter that make up everything in the Universe. Scientists study matter by breaking particles apart to find out about the smaller particles inside them.**

## *The first accelerator*

Machines called accelerators boost particles to higher speeds until they hit something and break apart. There are two types of **particle accelerator**. One makes particles go very fast in a straight line. These are called **linear accelerators**, or linacs. The other type of accelerator makes particles go round in circles, getting faster all the time. The first accelerator was a linear accelerator. It was made in 1928 by Norwegian engineer Rolf Wideröe.

Computer models show what happens when particles collide in an accelerator.

An atom has a nucleus in the middle with electrons flying around it.

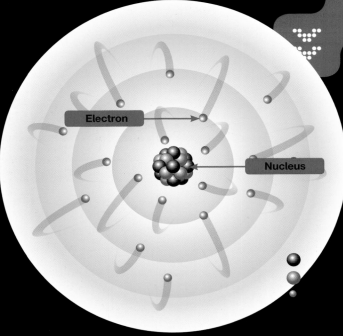

Electron

Nucleus

## DID YOU KNOW?

In 1932, British scientists John Cockcroft and Ernest Walton used a more powerful linear accelerator to probe particles of matter for the first time. They were awarded the Nobel Prize in physics in 1951 for their work.

Before the Large Hadron Collider, the most powerful particle accelerator in the world was the Tevatron at Fermilab. It was built inside an underground tunnel, measuring 3.7 miles.

## *Flying in circles*

Accelerators that make particles fly in circles can boost them to higher speeds than linear accelerators. These machines are called cyclotrons and synchrotrons. The first circular accelerator was a cyclotron built by Ernest O Lawrence in 1929.

The Large Hadron Collider is 69 feet long and weighs 12,500 tons! This huge structure is an instrument for studying particles inside it.

## *Max power*

The most powerful particle accelerator in the world is the Large Hadron Collider (LHC) at the European nuclear research centre, CERN. The LHC is built inside a tunnel that goes in a circle for 16.7 miles. It accelerates two streams of particles in opposite directions until they smash into each other.

# ROBOTS

**Clockwork models of birds and animals have been made for hundreds of years. They weren't called robots—the word robot was not invented until 1921.**

Computer-controlled mechanical arms do a lot of the work in car factories today.

## Industrial robots

Robots used in factories are called industrial robots. Most of them are mechanical arms that do work such as moving objects, drilling, welding, and painting. The first industrial robots were made in the United States in the 1950s. In 1956, George Devol and Joseph Engelberger started the first company in the world for building robots. Their first industrial robot, called Unimate, was used by the U.S. car maker, General Motors, in 1961.

Robots take part in a football competition in China.

## Going for a walk

Getting a robot to walk on two legs is very difficult. Humans do it without thinking, but getting a machine to walk without falling over involves tricky balancing and shifting weight from foot to foot. That's why most robots are bolted to the floor or move about on tracks or wheels. The first walking robot, called WABOT-1, was built at Waseda University in Tokyo, Japan, in 1973.

## *Amazing Asimo*

In 2000, Honda built a walking robot, Asimo. It looks like a small astronaut wearing a backpack. In 2005, Honda built a more advanced Asimo, capable of doing useful jobs in a real office. It can walk, run, carry things, remember people's faces, and even work as a receptionist or guide.

Honda's Asimo robot stands 4.2 feet tall and weighs 120 pounds.

## DID YOU KNOW?

U.S. writer and scientist Isaac Asimov invented three laws that robots should obey.

Law 1: A robot may not injure a human or, by inaction, allow a human to come to harm.

Law 2: A robot must obey orders from a human unless they would make it break the first law.

Law 3: A robot must protect itself unless that would break the first or second law.

ASIMO

HONDA

# GENETIC ENGINEERING

**Genetic engineering is one of the most exciting branches of science and technology today. It lets scientists change plants and animals, especially in farming and medicine.**

## Instructions for life

Everyone has a set of instructions, or a genetic code, inside their cells. The code tells your body how to grow and work. Your genetic code is different from everyone else's, apart from an identical twin. Identical twins have the same genetic code. The code is made of a substance called **DNA**.

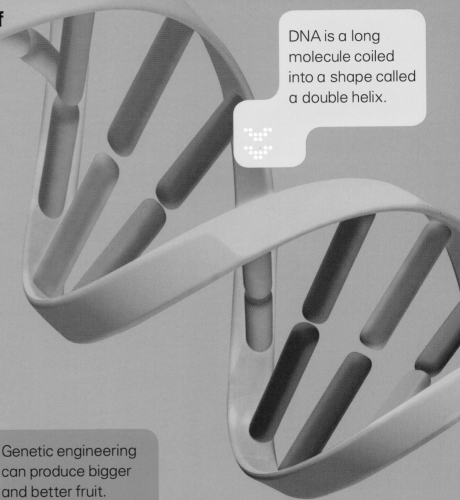

DNA is a long molecule coiled into a shape called a double helix.

Genetic engineering can produce bigger and better fruit.

## Changing the code

In some parts of the world, it is difficult to grow enough food because the soil is poor or the weather is too dry or too wet. Changing the genetic code of rice, wheat, or other plants grown for food invents new plants that are able to live better in these conditions. Some farm animals produce more milk or more meat than others. Using their DNA to produce new animals enables farmers to produce more milk and meat.

## *Making copies*

Scientists can now make identical copies of a plant or animal. All they need is one cell. They make the cell divide again and again to make lots of cells, which grow into a new plant or animal. This is called cloning and was invented in the 1950s. It is used to make identical copies of cells for research. Whole animals including sheep, pigs, goats, and cows have been cloned, too.

## DID YOU KNOW?

If the DNA in all of the 100 million million cells in your body was laid end to end, it would stretch all the way to the Sun (93 million miles away) and back more than 600 times!

Dolly the sheep was created in 1996. Dolly was a special clone—the first sheep to be grown from one cell taken from another fully grown sheep.

## GENETIC ENGINEERING TIMELINE

**1952** U.S. scientists Robert Briggs and Thomas King create the first clones of an animal.

**1953** U.S. scientist James Watson and English scientist Francis Crick work out how DNA particles fit together and what shape DNA is.

**1973** Genetic engineering begins.

**1978** Louise Brown, the first test-tube baby is born.

**1990** Scientists find the gene that makes babies develop as boys.

**1990** An illness is treated for the first time with genes. This is called gene therapy.

**1991** A sheep with some human genes is born. She produces substances in her milk that can be used to treat sick people.

**1994** A genetically modified tomato goes on sale. It is tastier and stays fresh for longer.

**2003** The Human Genome Project finishes its map of the human genetic code.

# GENETIC FINGERPRINTS

An invention called a genetic fingerprint, or DNA profile, has caused a major change in crime fighting. Using small drops of blood or strands of hair found at the scene of a crime, a genetic fingerprint can help to show who committed the crime.

## Comparing DNA

DNA found at a **crime scene** may belong to the person who committed the crime. Genetic fingerprints let scientists compare DNA from a crime scene with DNA collected from people arrested by the police to see if they match.

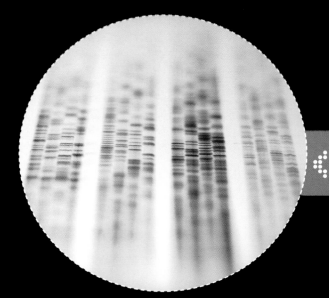

A genetic fingerprint looks like columns of lines on a piece of film or a computer screen.

Sir Alec Jeffreys checks a genetic fingerprint.

## Guilty or not guilty

Genetic fingerprinting was invented by British scientist Dr Alec Jeffreys at the University of Leicester, England, in 1984. It has helped the police to catch hundreds of criminals. It has also helped to prove that some people accused of crimes, or in prison, are not guilty.

Forensic scientists must be careful not to contaminate samples when working on them in the laboratory.

## *Paper suits*

When genetic fingerprinting was invented, a new way of gathering **evidence** at crime scenes had to be invented, too. A criminal often leaves DNA at the scene of a crime. Police officers and scientists who visit the scene could do the same thing. Their DNA could contaminate, or spoil, the evidence. So, investigators at the scenes of the most serious crimes have to wear paper suits, face masks and gloves.

## DID YOU KNOW?

DNA can last a very long time after a plant or animal dies. The oldest DNA ever found is at least 450,000 years old! It was found under 2,380 feet of ice in Greenland. The ancient DNA shows that icy Greenland was once warmer.

# FUTURE SCI-TECH

There are some parts of science and technology where great advances are being made now and more inventions are sure to follow in the future. They include genetics, robots, and a new technology called nanotechnology.

### Tiny technology

Nanotechnology makes things so small that you need a microscope to see them! It's called nanotechnology because "nano" means one billionth, and nano-machines are measured in nanometers. A nanometer is one billionth of a meter. Your fingernails grow about a nanometer in a second. As well as making tiny machines, special materials and surfaces can be built up particle by particle by using nanotechnology.

Future nano-machines may be designed to travel through our blood vessels to fix problems in our bodies.

Robot vacuum cleaners already work in some homes. Future robots may do more of the housework for us.

### Robots

Robots can already walk, talk, see, and hear, and they work in some offices, factories, and hospitals. In the future, they are likely to take over more of the jobs done by people today. New robots will be able to do things that people can't do. Some will be able to see in the dark. Others may have three or four hands instead of just two. Using robots with extra powers may lead to many new inventions.

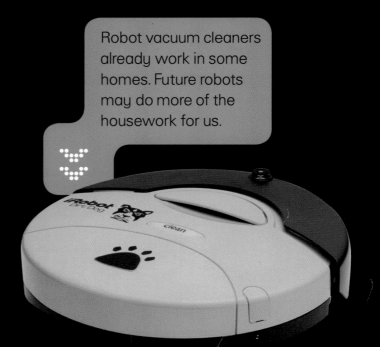

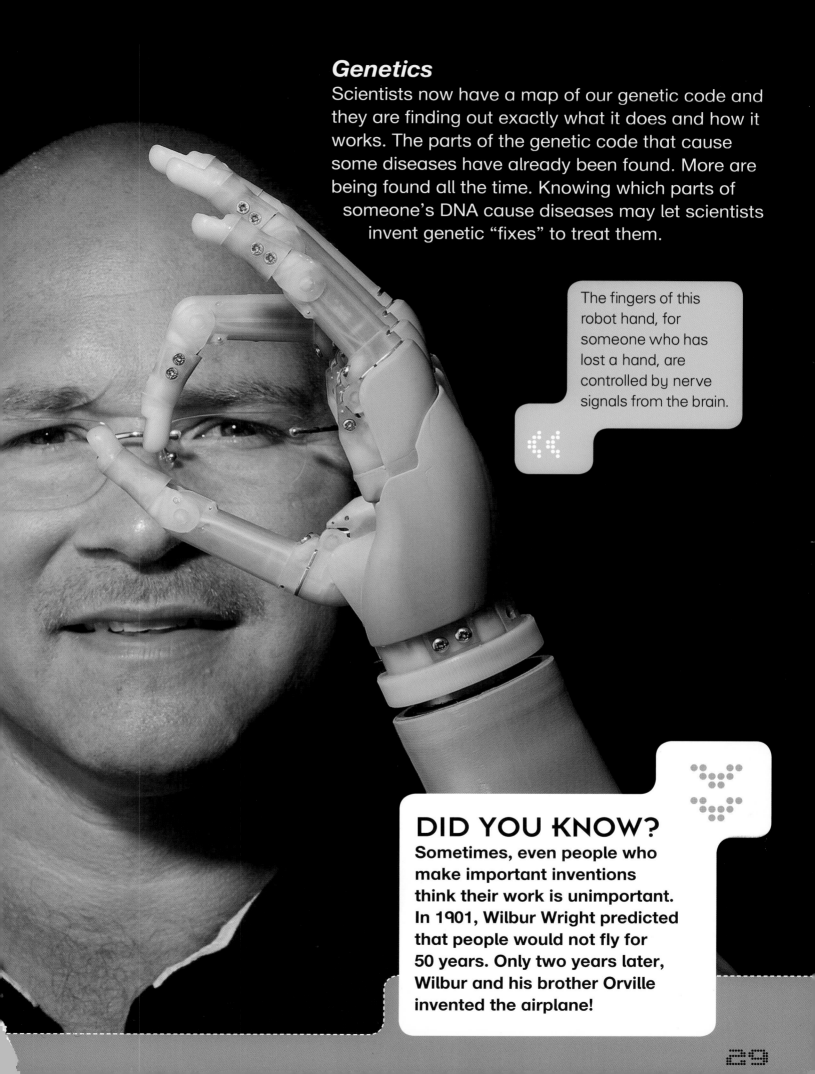

## Genetics

Scientists now have a map of our genetic code and they are finding out exactly what it does and how it works. The parts of the genetic code that cause some diseases have already been found. More are being found all the time. Knowing which parts of someone's DNA cause diseases may let scientists invent genetic "fixes" to treat them.

The fingers of this robot hand, for someone who has lost a hand, are controlled by nerve signals from the brain.

## DID YOU KNOW?

Sometimes, even people who make important inventions think their work is unimportant. In 1901, Wilbur Wright predicted that people would not fly for 50 years. Only two years later, Wilbur and his brother Orville invented the airplane!

# GLOSSARY

**Astronaut**
A person who travels in space.

**Atom**
The smallest part of a substance that can exist on its own and take part in chemical reactions.

**Cell**
The smallest part of a living thing that can work on its own or with other cells. Plants and animals are made of different types of cell that do different things. The cells in a human body include skin cells, muscle cells, and liver cells.

**Concave**
A round, hollowed-out shape, like the inside of a bowl.

**Convex**
A rounded shape that bulges outward, like the outside of a bowl.

**Crime scene**
The place where a crime was carried out.

**DNA**
The material that makes up the genetic code inside living cells. DNA stands for deoxyribonucleic acid.

**Electron**
One of the particles found inside an atom.

**Electron microscope**
An instrument that uses a beam of electrons to make a greatly magnified picture of something.

**Energy**
The ability to do work. There are different types of energy, including heat, light, and electrical energy.

**Evidence**
Facts that prove something. In crime-fighting science, evidence is collected from the scene of a crime to help show what happened and who might have done it.

**Generator**
A machine that makes electricity.

**Gravity**
A force that pulls everything toward the Earth or any other large object. Gravity pulls you down toward the ground. The Sun's gravity keeps all the planets flying around the Sun and moons flying around planets.

## Laser
An instrument that produces an intense beam of very pure light.

## Lens
A piece of glass shaped so that it bends light rays to make an image. One side of a lens is curved. The other side may be flat or curved.

## Linear accelerator
A particle accelerator that makes pieces of matter go very fast in a straight line so that scientists can study them.

## Magnify
To make something look bigger.

## Matter
The material something is made of. Matter is made of particles called atoms, and atoms themselves are made of even smaller particles.

## Microscope
An instrument that makes very small things look bigger.

## Nuclear reactor
The place where nuclear energy produces heat.

## Particle accelerator
A machine for making tiny pieces of matter go very fast and crash into each other so that scientists can study what happens to them.

## Robot
A machine that does things a human being usually does.

## Spacecraft
Manned or unmanned vehicles that fly in space.

## Space station
A manned spacecraft that stays in space and is visited by a series of crews from Earth.

## Supercomputers
The fastest computers in the world.

# Index